GRADE

Success With

Grammar

■ SCHOLASTIC

Editor: Ourania Papacharalambous
Cover design by Tannaz Fassihi; cover illustration by Kevin Zimmer
Interior design by Mina Chen
Interior illustrations by Doug Jones (3, 17-19, 27, 33, 40, 42); all other illustrations by Maarten Lenoir

ISBN 978-1-338-79837-1
Scholastic Inc., 557 Broadway, New York, NY 10012
Copyright © 2022 Scholastic Inc.
All rights reserved. Printed in the U.S.A.
First printing, January 2022
1 2 3 4 5 6 7 8 9 10   40   29 28 27 26 25 24 23 22

INTRODUCTION

No other resource boosts grammar skills like *Scholastic Success With Grammar*! For classroom or at-home use, this exciting series for grades 1 through 5 provides invaluable reinforcement and practice in grammar topics such as sentence types, verb tenses, parts of speech, subject-verb agreement, common and proper nouns, punctuation, sentence structure, capitalization, and more!

This 48-page book contains loads of clever practice pages to keep kids challenged and excited as they strengthen the grammar skills they need to read and write well. On page 4, you will find a list of the key skills covered in the activities throughout this book. Each practice page reinforces a specific, age-appropriate skill. What's more, the activities for each skill are followed by an assessment sheet that gives children realistic practice in taking tests—and gives you a useful tool to follow their progress!

Take the lead and help children succeed with *Scholastic Success With Grammar*. Parents and teachers agree: No one helps children succeed like Scholastic.

TABLE OF CONTENTS

Grade-Appropriate Skills Covered in *Scholastic Success With Grammar: Grade I*

Demonstrate understanding of the organization and basic features of print.

Recognize the distinguishing features of a sentence.

Know and apply grade-level phonics and word analysis skills in decoding words.

Decode regularly spelled one-syllable words.

Read words with inflectional endings.

Recognize and read grade-appropriate irregularly spelled words.

Read with sufficient accuracy and fluency to support comprehension.

Demonstrate command of the conventions of standard English grammar and usage when writing or speaking.

Print all upper- and lowercase letters.

Use common, proper, and possessive nouns.

Use singular and plural nouns with matching verbs in basic sentences.

Use personal, possessive, and indefinite pronouns.

Use verbs to convey a sense of past, present, and future.

Use frequently occurring adjectives.

Produce and expand complete simple and compound declarative, interrogative, imperative, and exclamatory sentences in response to prompts.

Demonstrate command of the conventions of standard English capitalization, punctuation, and spelling when writing.

Capitalize dates and names of people.

Use end punctuation for sentences.

With guidance and support from adults, demonstrate understanding of word relationships and nuances in word meanings.

Capitalize Names

Circle the special names in the picture.
Write each one correctly on a line.

Words that name a special person, place, animal, or thing begin with a capital letter.

1 _____

- - - - - - - - - - - - - - - -

_____

3 _____

- - - - - - - - - - - - - - - -

_____

2 _____

- - - - - - - - - - - - - - - -

_____

4 _____

- - - - - - - - - - - - - - - -

_____

Capitalize Names and First Words

Read the sentences.
Circle the words that are capitalized.

1 The goats have a problem.

2 They do not like the troll.

3 The troll's name is Nosey.

4 Nosey is big and bad.

> The first word in a sentence begins with a capital letter. Words that name a special person, place, animal, or thing also begin with a capital letter.

. . . .

Draw a line to match each sentence to why the underlined word is capitalized.

1 Dan and <u>Pam</u> like the play.

2 <u>They</u> will read it to Jim.

First word in a sentence

Names a special person, place, animal, or thing

Capitalize Names and First Words

Read each sentence. Fill in the circle next to the word that needs a capital letter.

1 the goats went for a walk.
- ○ Goats
- ○ The
- ○ Walk

2 I read the story with ron.
- ○ Read
- ○ Story
- ○ Ron

3 Little billy had a problem.
- ○ Had
- ○ Billy
- ○ Problem

4 a troll was on the bridge.
- ○ On
- ○ Bridge
- ○ A

5 The troll's name was nosey.
- ○ Name
- ○ Nosey
- ○ His

Periods

Circle the period at the end of each sentence.

1 I see Jan.

2 We see Dan.

3 I go with Jan.

4 I go with Dan and Jan.

Draw a line under the last word in each sentence.
Add a period to each sentence.

1 We go to school

2 We like school

Periods

Add a period where it belongs in each sentence.
Read the sentences to a friend.

1 Dan is in the cab

2 The cat is in the cab

3 Mom is in the cab

4 We see Dan and Mom

· ·

Read the words. Write each word at the end of the correct sentence.

van.	red.

1 We can go in the _____

2 The van is _____

Periods

Read each group of words.
Fill in the circle next to the sentence that is written correctly.

1 ○ The cat is on the mat.
○ the cat is on the mat
○ the cat on the mat

2 ○ The rat sees the cat
○ The rat sees the cat.
○ the rat sees the cat

3 ○ the cat and rat sit
○ The cat and rat sit
○ The cat and rat sit.

4 ○ the rat is on the mat
○ the rat is on the mat.
○ The rat is on the mat.

5 ○ The rat can hop.
○ The rat can hop
○ the rat can hop

Capitalize *I*

Always write the word *I* with a capital letter.

Circle the word *I* in each sentence.

1 I like to hop.

2 I can hop to Mom.

3 Pam and I like to hop.

4 Mom and I can hop.

Draw what you like. Use the word *I* to write about it.

_____

_____

_____

Capitalize *I*

Read the sentences. Write *I* on the line.

_____

1 _____ will ride.

_____

3 Dad and _____ will sing.

_____

2 _____ will swim.

_____

4 Then _____ will read.

What will you do next? Write it on the line.

I will _____.

Capitalize *I*

Read each group of words.
Fill in the circle next to the sentence that is written correctly.

1 ○ i sit on a mat.
○ I sit on a mat.
○ i sit on a mat

2 ○ I see the van.
○ i see the van.
○ i see the van

3 ○ i like to nap.
○ I like to nap.
○ i like to nap

4 ○ Pam and I like cats.
○ Pam and i like cats.
○ pam and i like cats

5 ○ i like jam.
○ i like jam
○ I like jam.

6 ○ i like the park
○ I like the park.
○ I like the park

Simple Sentences

A sentence tells a complete idea.

Circle who or what each sentence is about.

1 Pam ran.

2 Dan hops.

3 The cat sits.

4 The van can go.

Draw a line from each sentence to the picture of who or what the sentence is about.

1 Jon is hot.

2 The hat is on top.

3 The man sat.

Simple Sentences

Circle each sentence.

1 Bill

Bill paints.

3 plants flowers

Paul plants flowers.

2 likes to read

Tom likes to read.

4 cooks

Leon cooks.

Finish the sentence.

I like   .

Simple Sentences

Read each group of words.
Fill in the circle next to the complete sentence.

1 ○ on a mat
○ The cat sits on a mat.
○ The cat

2 ○ I see Mom.
○ I see
○ Mom

3 ○ Ben
○ Ben can hop.
○ hop

4 ○ Pam and Dan like jam.
○ Pam and Dan
○ like jam

5 ○ my hat
○ I like
○ I like my hat.

6 ○ Dina rides a bike.
○ Dina bike.
○ rides a bike

Word Order

Read each group of words. Draw a line under the word that should go first in each sentence.

> Words in a sentence must be in an order that makes sense.

1 dots. I like

3 Pam dots. likes

2 like We hats.

4 hats with dots. We like

Write each group of words from above in the correct order.

1 _____

2 _____

3 _____

4 _____

Word Order

These words are mixed up.
Write them in the correct order on the lines.

1 snow. bear likes This

_____

- -

_____

2 water cold. The is

_____

- -

_____

3 fast. The runs bear

_____

- -

_____

4 play. bears Two

_____

- -

_____

Word Order

Read each group of words. Fill in the circle next to the words that are in an order that makes sense.

1 ○ Pam will bake a cake.
○ bake Pam a will cake.
○ will Pam cake. a bake

2 ○ duck. The king has a
○ The king has a duck.
○ has a king The duck.

3 ○ The king will eat cake.
○ king will The cake. eat
○ cake. king will The eat

4 ○ will king. the see Pam
○ king. Pam see will the
○ Pam will see the king.

5 ○ lake. the in is The duck
○ The duck is in the lake.
○ The lake. duck in is the

6 ○ Ramón will help Pam bake.
○ bake. Ramón help will Pam
○ Ramón bake. Pam will help

Question Sentences

Read each sentence. Circle each question mark.

> A question sentence asks something. It ends with a question mark. (?)

1 Who hid the hat?

2 Is it on the cat?

3 Can you see the hat?

4 Is it on the man?

· ·

Write two questions. Draw a line under each capital letter at the beginning of each question. Circle the question marks.

1 _____

2 _____

Question Sentences

Draw a line under each sentence that asks a question.
Circle the question mark.

1 Who hid the cat?

2 Can the cat see the rat?

3 The cat is in the van.

4 Can the van go?

Read the sentences. Circle each sentence that asks something.

1 Can we sit in the van?

We can sit in the van.

2 Dan can nap in the van.

Can Dan nap in the van?

Question Sentences

Read the sentences. Fill in the circle next to the sentence that asks a question.

1 ○ Who hid my hat?
○ My hat is with him.
○ My hat is big.

2 ○ The hat has spots.
○ The hat has dots.
○ Does the hat have dots?

3 ○ Can you see the hat?
○ You can see the hat.
○ She can see the hat.

4 ○ Jan likes my hat.
○ Does Jan like my hat?
○ Jan does like my hat.

5 ○ Dan can get a hat.
○ Dan likes hats.
○ Did Dan get a hat?

Naming Words

Read each sentence. Draw a line under the naming words.

> A naming word names a person, place, animal, or thing.

① We play at school.

② The girl kicks.

③ The ball is fast.

④ The friends run.

Circle the naming words that belong in each list.
Cross out the word that does not belong.

Person	Place	Animal	Thing
girl	home	dog	Pam
school	school	man	cup
Jonah	Bill	rabbit	ball

Naming Words

Circle the naming words in the sentences.

1 Al can go in a van.

2 The cat sat on a mat.

3 Pat ran up the hill.

4 Dan and Jan will mop.

Draw a picture of a person, place, animal, or thing.
Write a sentence about your picture. Circle the naming word.

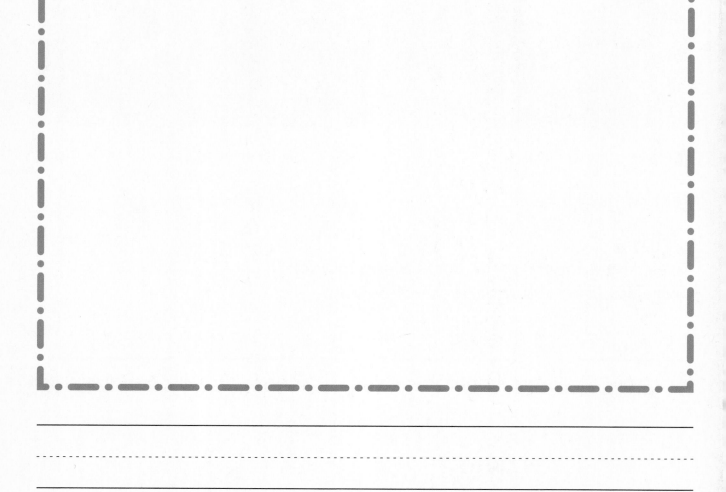

_____

- -

_____

Naming Words

Read each sentence. Fill in the circle next to the word that names a person, place, animal, or thing.

1. Who plays in the park?
   - ○ play
   - ○ Let's
   - ○ park

2. The friends laugh and play.
   - ○ friends
   - ○ the
   - ○ kick

3. The net is new.
   - ○ get
   - ○ net
   - ○ jump

4. The girl can run and kick.
   - ○ girl
   - ○ run
   - ○ kick

5. The boy can jump.
   - ○ can
   - ○ jump
   - ○ boy

Capitalize Special Names

Draw a line under the special name in each sentence. Then circle the first letter or letters in that name.

The names of specific people, places, and pets are special. They begin with capital letters.

① They go to Hill Park.

② Don sees the cat.

③ Pam sees the ham.

④ They like Frog Lake.

....

Write the special name of a person, place, or pet you know.

_____

- -

_____

Capitalize Special Names

Circle each special name in the sentences below.
Then, draw a line under each capital letter in the special names.

1 I am Pam.

2 Ron likes the lake.

3 I sit on Ant Hill.

4 He likes Bat Lake.

· ·

Read the special names in the box.
Write the special name for each picture.

| Spot | Hill Street |

1

_____

- -

_____

2

_____

- -

_____

Capitalize Special Names

Read each sentence. Fill in the circle next to the special name.

1 Can Don go to the picnic?
  ○ picnic
  ○ Don
  ○ Can

2 The picnic will be
on Pig Hill.
  ○ Pig Hill
  ○ picnic
  ○ The

3 Jan will go to the picnic.
  ○ go
  ○ picnic
  ○ Jan

4 The hill is on Jam Street.
  ○ hill
  ○ The
  ○ Jam Street

5 She will go to Ham Lake.
  ○ She
  ○ Ham Lake
  ○ will

Action Words

Read each sentence.
Circle the word that tells what happens.

1 The hen sits.

2 The dog digs.

3 Mom sees the hen.

4 The cat naps.

....

Read the action words. Use them to finish the sentences.

sees	run

_____

- -

1 She _____ eggs.

_____

- -

2 It can _____ fast.

Action Words

Look at the pictures. Read the action words in the box.
Write the correct action word on the line.

talk	play	dance	run

_____

- -

1 Sue and Al _____ ball.

_____

- -

2 The bears _____ .

_____

- -

3 Rabbit and Pig _____ .

_____

- -

4 Tami and Lee _____ fast.

Action Words

Read each sentence. Fill in the circle next to the action word.

1 The hen sits.
- ○ hen
- ○ sits
- ○ The

2 The green frog hops.
- ○ frog
- ○ green
- ○ hops

3 The big pig ran.
- ○ big
- ○ pig
- ○ ran

4 The cat naps in the van.
- ○ naps
- ○ cat
- ○ van

5 The dog digs.
- ○ digs
- ○ dog
- ○ The

6 The cute kitten jumps.
- ○ jumps
- ○ cute
- ○ The

Describing Words

A describing word tells more about a person, place, animal, or thing.

Read each sentence. Circle the word in each sentence that describes the cat.

1. I see a big cat.

2. The fast cat ran.

3. My cat is bad.

4. The fat cat naps.

· ·

Look at each cat. Circle the word that describes it.

1

big   little

2

big   little

Describing Words

Look at each picture. Circle the words that describes it.

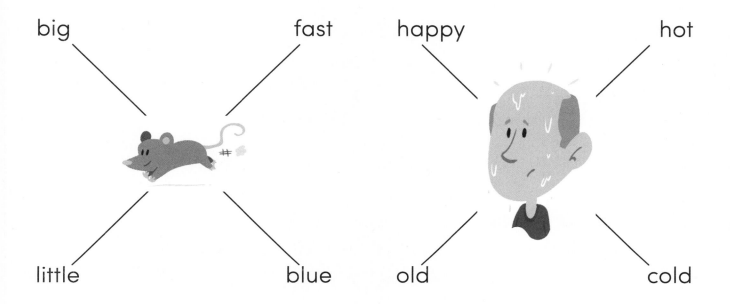

big   fast   happy   hot

little   blue   old   cold

Draw a line between each sentence and the picture that shows what it describes.

1 It is fat.

2 They are little.

Describing Words

Read each sentence. Fill in the circle next to the describing word.

1 The silly cat can play.
○ silly
○ cat
○ play

2 The black dog naps.
○ dog
○ black
○ naps

3 A green frog can hop.
○ frog
○ green
○ hop

4 The fast rat ran.
○ fast
○ ran
○ rat

5 The cow is big.
○ cow
○ is
○ big

6 The gray cat sleeps.
○ cat
○ sleeps
○ gray

Telling Sentences

Circle the capital letter at the beginning of each telling sentence. Then circle the period at the end of each telling sentence.

1 I see the basket.

2 The cat is in the basket.

3 Hats can go in it.

4 The sock can go in it.

Draw a line under each telling sentence.

1 I can fill the basket.

2 Can you get the mop?

3 We can clean.

4 Do you like the vase?

5 He jogs on Mondays.

6 She helps her father cook.

Telling Sentences

Draw a line to match each sentence with the picture that shows what the sentence tells.

1 She has a mop.

2 The dog is on top.

3 Dan gets the hats.

4 Ron can clean spots.

. . . .

Read the sentences.
Circle the capital letter and period in the telling sentence.

1 Put it in the pot.   **2** Is it in the pan?

Telling Sentences

Read the sentences. Fill in the circle next to each telling sentence.

1 ○ Can you get the basket?
 ○ You can get it.
 ○ Can you fill it?

2 ○ What can go in it?
 ○ Will the hat go in?
 ○ The hat is in the basket.

3 ○ Can we fill it?
 ○ We can fill the basket.
 ○ Will you fill it?

4 ○ The basket is small.
 ○ Is the basket big?
 ○ Why is it big?

5 ○ A cat cannot go in it.
 ○ Can a cat go in?
 ○ Will a cat go in it?

6 ○ Can the toys go in
   the basket?
 ○ I put the toys in the basket.
 ○ What is in the basket?

Exclamation Sentences

Read each sentence. Circle each exclamation mark. Draw a line under the capital letter at the beginning of each sentence.

> Exclamation sentences show strong feelings, such as excitement, surprise, or fear. They end with exclamation marks. (!)

1 Help! The cat is on top!

2 Get the cat!

3 This cat is bad!

4 Uh-oh! The cat is wet!

· ·

Read each set of sentences. Draw a line under the sentence or sentences that show strong feeling.

1 Oh, my! Get the dog!

   Let's get the dog.

2 The dog runs.

   Oh! The dog runs!

Exclamation Sentences

Choose the sentence in each pair that shows strong feeling.
Write it on the line. Put an exclamation mark at the end.

1 Run to the show   We will go to the show

_____

2 I'm late for it   Oh, my, I'm very late

_____

3 What a great show   I liked the show

_____

4 The floor is wet   Watch out, the floor is wet

_____

5 We had fun   Wow, we had lots of fun

_____

Exclamation Sentences

Read each group of sentences. Fill in the circle next to the sentence or sentences that show strong feeling.

1 ○ The cow is on the hill.
○ The cow likes grass.
○ Yes! The cow can kick!

2 ○ The rat will run.
○ That rat runs fast!
○ The rat can hop.

3 ○ The pot can get hot.
○ The pot is hot!
○ Fill the pot with mud.

4 ○ That cat is bad!
○ That cat naps.
○ Is the cat on the mat?

5 ○ Oh, no! A frog is in my house!
○ A frog hops.
○ The frog is green.

Singular/Plural Nouns

Many nouns, or naming words, add -s to show more than one. Words that show more than one are called *plurals*.

Read each sentence. Draw a line under each naming word that means more than one.

1 I see hats and a cap.

2 The girls swim.

3 It sits on eggs.

4 Pam can pet cats.

. . . .

Read each sentence. Write the plural naming word on the line.

_____

1 The mugs are hot.   _____

_____

2 Mud is on my hands.   _____

Singular/Plural Nouns

Read each set of sentences. Draw a line under the sentence that has a naming word that names more than one.

1 Jan has her mittens.

Jan has her mitten.

2 Jan runs with her dog.

Jan runs with her dogs.

3 She will run up a hill.

She will run up hills.

4 The dogs can jump.

The dog can jump.

- -

Look at each picture. Read each word.
Write the plural naming word that matches the picture.

 **1** cat _____

_____

 **2** sock _____

_____

Singular/Plural Nouns

Read each sentence. Fill in the circle next to the plural naming word.

1 Jim gets mud on his hands.
- ○ gets
- ○ hands
- ○ mud

2 The dogs dig fast.
- ○ dig
- ○ fast
- ○ dogs

3 The frogs hop.
- ○ The
- ○ frogs
- ○ hop

4 Pam can fill the pots with mud.
- ○ pots
- ○ mud
- ○ fill

5 The ants are on the plant.
- ○ ants
- ○ plant
- ○ are

6 The kittens are on the sofa.
- ○ sofa
- ○ on
- ○ kittens

Linking Verbs

Read each sentence. Draw a line under the linking verb *is*, *are*, *was*, or *were*.

Is, are, was, and *were* are linking verbs. *Is* tells about one. *Are* tells about more than one. *Was* tells about one in the past. *Were* tells about more than one in the past.

1 The hen is digging.

2 The pig was having fun.

3 The chicks were helping.

4 The cat and duck are playing.

. . . .

Read each sentence. Circle *now* or *past* to show when it happens or happened.

1 The hen is planting.   **now**   **past**

2 The cat was not helping.   **now**   **past**

3 The chicks are with the hen.   **now**   **past**

Linking Verbs

Circle the linking verb. Write *now* or *past* to tell when the action happens or happened.

1 The chicks are eating. _____

2 The duck is swimming. _____

3 The cat was napping. _____

4 The pig is digging. _____

5 They were playing. _____

Linking Verbs

Fill in the circle next to the linking verb that completes each sentence.

1 The hen _____ sitting.
○ was
○ are
○ were

2 The pigs _____ digging.
○ was
○ is
○ are

3 The chicks _____ napping.
○ was
○ is
○ are

4 They _____ playing.
○ were
○ is
○ was

5 The duck _____ swimming.
○ were
○ is
○ are

6 The cat _____ meowing.
○ are
○ were
○ is

ANSWER KEY

Page 5
1. Raul 2. Ms. Chin
3. Sue 4. Mr. Poh

Page 6
1. The 2. They
3. The, Nosey 4. Nosey
1. Dan and Pam like the play.
Names a special person, place,
animal, or thing
2. They will read it to Jim.
First word in a sentence

Page 7
1. The 2. Ron 3. Billy
4. A 5. Nosey

Page 8
1. I see Jan⊙
2. We see Dan⊙
3. I go with Jan⊙
4. I go with Dan and Jan⊙
1. school. 2. school.

Page 9
1—4. Add a period to the end of
each sentence.
1. van. 2. red.

Page 10
1. The cat is on the mat.
2. The rat sees the cat.
3. The cat and rat sit.
4. The rat is on the mat.
5. The rat can hop.

Page 11
1. Ⓘ like to hop.
2. Ⓘ can hop to Mom.
3. Pam and Ⓘ like to hop.
4. Mom and Ⓘ can hop.
Pictures and sentences will vary.

Page 12
1—4. Write *I* on the lines.
Answers will vary.

Page 13
1. I sit on a mat.
2. I see the van.
3. I like to nap.
4. Pam and I like cats.
5. I like jam.
6. I like the park.

Page 14
1. Pam 2. Dan
3. The cat 4. The van

1. Jon is hot.
2. The hat is on top.
3. The man sat.

Page 15
1. Bill paints.
2. Tom likes to read.
3. Paul plants flowers.
4. Leon cooks.
Sentences will vary.

Page 16
1. The cat sits on a mat.
2. I see Mom.
3. Ben can hop.
4. Pam and Dan like jam.
5. I like my hat.
6. Dina rides a bike.

Page 17
1. I 2. We 3. Pam 4. We
1. I like dots.
2. We like hats.
3. Pam likes dots.
4. We like hats with dots.

Page 18
1. This bear likes snow.
2. The water is cold.
3. The bear runs fast.
4. Two bears play.

Page 19
1. Pam will bake a cake.
2. The king has a duck.
3. The king will eat cake.
4. Pam will see the king.
5. The duck is in the lake.
6. Ramón will help Pam bake.

Page 20
1. ⑦ 2. ⑦ 3. ⑦ 4. ⑦
Questions will vary.

Page 21
1. Who hid the cat⑦
2. Can the cat see the rat⑦
4. Can the van go⑦
1. Can we sit in the van?
2. Can Dan nap in the van?

Page 22
1. Who hid my hat?
2. Does the hat have dots?
3. Can you see the hat?
4. Does Jan like my hat?
5. Did Dan get a hat?

Page 23
1. We, school 2. girl
3. ball 4. friends
Person: girl, ~~school,~~ Jonah
Place: home, school, ~~Bill~~
Animal: dog, ~~man,~~ rabbit
Thing: ~~Pam,~~ cup, ball

Page 24
1. Al, van 2. cat, mat
3. Pat, hill 4. Dan, Jan
Pictures and sentences will vary.

Page 25
1. park 2. friends 3. net
4. girl 5. boy

Page 26
1. (H)ill (P)ark 2. (D)on
3. (P)am 4. (F)rog (L)ake
Answers will vary.

Page 27
1. (Pam) 2. (Ron)
3. (Ant Hill) 4. (Bat Lake)
1. Spot 2. Hill Street

Page 28
1. Don 2. Pig Hill 3. Jan
4. Jam Street 5. Ham Lake

Page 29
1. sits 2. digs 3. sees 4. naps
1. sees 2. run

Page 30
1. play 2. dance 3. talk 4. run

Page 31
1. sits 2. hops 3. ran
4. naps 5. digs 6. jumps

Page 32
1. big 2. fast 3. bad 4. fat
1. big 2. little

Page 33
1. little, fast 2. hot, old

1. It is fat.
2. They are little.

Page 34
1. silly 2. black 3. green
4. fast 5. big 6. gray

Page 35
1. (I) see the basket ⊙
2. (T)he cat is in the basket ⊙
3. (H)ats can go in it ⊙
4. (T)he sock can go in it ⊙
1. I can fill the basket.
3. We can clean.
5. He jogs on Mondays.
6. She helps her father cook.

Page 36
1. She has a mop.
2. The dog is on top.
3. Dan gets the hats.
4. Ron can clean spots.
1. (P)ut it in the pot ⊙

Page 37
1. You can get it.
2. The hat is in the basket.
3. We can fill the basket.
4. The basket is small.
5. A cat cannot go in it.
6. I put the toys in the basket.

Page 38
1. Help (!) The cat is on top (!)
2. Get the cat (!)
3. This cat is bad (!)
4. Uh-oh (!) The cat is wet (!)
1. Oh, my! Get the dog!
2. Oh! The dog runs!

Page 39
1. Run to the show!
2. Oh, my, I'm very late!
3. What a great show!
4. Watch out, the floor is wet!
5. Wow, we had lots of fun!

Page 40
1. Yes! The cow can kick!
2. That rat runs fast!
3. The pot is hot!
4. That cat is bad!
5. Oh, no! A frog is in my house!

Page 41
1. hats 2. girls
3. eggs 4. cats
1. mugs 2. hands

Page 42
1. Jan has her mittens.
2. Jan runs with her dogs.
3. She will run up hills.
4. The dogs can jump.
1. cats 2. socks

Page 43
1. hands 2. dogs 3. frogs
4. pots 5. ants 6. kittens

Page 44
1. is 2. was 3. were 4. are
1. now 2. past 3. now

Page 45
1. (are) now 2. (is) now
3. (was) past 4. (is) now
5. (were) past

Page 46
1. was 2. are 3. are
4. were 5. is 6. is